Where Have You Been?

by MARGARET WISE BROWN

Pictures by BARBARA COONEY

SCHOLASTIC BOOK SERVICES

NEW YORK • LONDON • RICHMOND HILL, ONTARIO

1st printing .... September 1965

Printed in the U.S.A.

More books by the same author and illustrator:

CHRISTMAS IN THE BARN
THE LITTLE FIR TREE

Little Old Cat
Little Old Cat
Where have you been?
To see this and that
Said the Little Old Cat
That's where I've been.

Little Old Squirrel
Little Old Squirrel
Where have you been?
I've been out on a whirl
Said the Little Old Squirrel
That's where I've been.

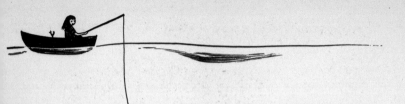

Little Old Fish
Little Old Fish
Where do you swim?
Wherever I wish
Said the Little Old Fish
That's where I swim.

Little Brown Bird
Little Brown Bird
Where do you fly?
I fly in the sky
Said the Little Brown Bird
That's where I fly.

Little Old Horse
Little Old Horse
Where have you been?
In the clover, of course
Said the Little Old Horse
That's where I've been.

Little Old Toad
Little Old Toad
Where have you been?
I've been way up the road
Said the Little Old Toad
That's where I've been.

Little Old Frog
Little Old Frog
Where have you been?
I've been sitting on a log
Said the Little Old Frog
That's where I've been.

Little Old Mole
Little Old Mole
Where have you been?
Down a long dark hole
Said the Little Old Mole
That's where I've been.

Little Old Bee
Little Old Bee
Where have you been?
In a pink apple tree
Said the Little Old Bee
That's where I've been.

Little Old Whale
Little Old Whale
Where do you sail?
Down under the gale
Said the Little Old Whale
That's where I sail.

Little Old Bunny
Little Old Bunny
Why do you run?
I run because it's fun
Said the Little Old Bunny
That's why I run.

Little Old Lion
Little Old Lion
Where have you been?
Where the jungle grows dim
Said the Little Old Lion
That's where I've been.

Little Old Mouse
Little Old Mouse
Why run down the clock?
To see if the tick
Comes after the tock
I run down the clock.

Little Old Rook
Little Old Rook
Where do you look?
At the very last page
Of this very same book
Said the Little Old Rook.

Little Sister

By Kathleen N. Daly

Illustrated by Eugenie

A GOLDEN BOOK · NEW YORK

Western Publishing Company, Inc., Racine, Wisconsin 53404

Copyright © 1986 by Western Publishing Company, Inc. Illustrations copyright © 1986 by Eugenie Fernandes. All rights reserved. Printed in the U.S.A. No part of this book may be reproduced or copied in any form without written permission from the publisher. GOLDEN®, GOLDEN & DESIGN®, A GOLDEN BOOK®, and A BIG LITTLE GOLDEN BOOK® are trademarks of Western Publishing Company, Inc. Library of Congress Catalog Card Number: 85-51681   ISBN 0-307-10256-4/ISBN 0-307-68256-0 (lib. bdg.)
B C D E F G H I J

Liz did a perfect cartwheel on the white sand of the beach. Then she did another and another until she landed in the water.

Her brother, David, dived in after her and they splashed each other, shrieking and laughing.

David and Liz were good friends.

David helped his little sister put on her snorkel.

"Make sure the mask feels snug around your face," he said. "And hold the snorkel in your mouth, like this."

"I know, I know," mumbled Liz.

This was their first vacation on a tropical island, but already they had learned a lot.

David always swam close to Liz and sometimes held her hand.

He pointed out a beautiful piece of coral and some bright blue fish. He pulled her away from a cave when they saw the big head of a spotted eel watching them.

He warned her to steer clear of the black, spiny sea urchins on the bottom.

At night the two children lay in their cool beds. Sometimes David told Liz a story, or they made up stories together. But usually they were both so tired from the sun and the water that they fell asleep before the story was over.

One day some new kids came to the beach. They were a little older than David.

David went up to them and said, "Hi, I'm David. This is my sister, Liz."

"Hi, Dave," said the other kids.

"I'm Peter."

"I'm Sue. Can you swim?"

"Sure," said David. "Race you to the raft!"

All the children dashed into the water and started swimming.

Liz soon got left behind. She was a good swimmer, but she couldn't keep up with the older kids.

All of them were already on the raft when she reached it.

"Come on up, Slowpoke," said David, hauling her up.

David had never called her "Slowpoke" before.

"I am *not* a slowpoke," said Liz, and everyone laughed.

"Race you all back," said Peter.

Before Liz could catch her breath, they were in the water again and racing toward shore.

Liz was the last to arrive.

"Let's climb up those rocks," said Sue, and they ran off.
"Wait for me!" shouted Liz. "Dave!"
But David was rushing ahead to catch up with Peter.
"You're too small for our games," called Sue. "Don't be a pest!"

"I am *not* a pest," said Liz. "Am I, Dave?"
But nobody heard her. They were all too busy scrambling up the rocks.

Liz did her best to follow, but the rocks were too big for her.

"Hey, Liz," said David on his way down, "maybe you should go home now. We're going to see that big boat that belongs to Pete and Sue's dad. Go on home."

"I will not," said Liz.

"Oh, don't be a pest, Liz," said David, and off he went with the others.

Liz was hurt to hear David call her a pest. She felt tears prickle in her eyes. Then she ran off down the beach so nobody would see her cry.

But nobody looked back, not even David.

Liz did a couple of cartwheels and felt better.
She scuffed her toes in the sand and found a beautiful shell.
She walked into the water. It felt so good she lay down in it.
Then she floated on her stomach a little way out. She put
her face in the water with her eyes open. Through the clear,
shallow water she could see some spiny sea urchins. They
looked like big pincushions.

Liz was careful not to touch them. She knew the spines could break off and stick in her skin and hurt a lot. But she loved to watch the strange creatures, their spines waving with the gentle movement of the water.

Suddenly Liz saw two tiny pink feet near the bed of sea urchins. She lifted her face out of the water.

A baby was wading nearby, reaching toward the sea urchins.

"Stop!" Liz called.

She back-paddled until she was clear of the spines, then she stood up.

"Don't step on those spines," shouted Liz. "They can hurt you!"

"Hi," said the baby, with a big smile.

"You've got to stand still," she said to the baby. "Don't move!"

The baby stretched out his hands to her.

Carefully Liz stepped in among the sea urchins, trying to watch her feet and the baby at the same time.

"Don't move, don't move," she kept saying.

The baby just stared at her.

As soon as she was close enough, Liz leaned forward and swept the baby up into her arms. The baby giggled, and clutched at Liz's hair. Liz almost fell over, the baby was so heavy.

Liz started to step carefully toward the beach. Then the baby wriggled and Liz almost lost her balance. She had to put her foot down in a hurry.

"Ow ow ouch!" she screamed as she felt the prick of an urchin spine in her foot.

But she didn't let go of the baby until they reached the dry sand.

Now the beach seemed to be full of people.

"My baby, my baby!" screamed a woman, scooping up her child.

Peter and Sue and David came running.

"Oh, my goodness, it's Nicholas," said Sue. "We were supposed to keep an eye on him."

"Thanks, Liz," said Peter. "You saved our baby brother from the sea urchins. That was really brave."

"It sure was," said Sue.

David gave Liz a hug, then he took her foot and looked at it carefully.

"We've got to get home," he said. "I'll carry you piggyback."

"Does that make me a pest?" asked Liz.

David bent down so she could climb on his back.

"Yes," he said with a grin. "But you're a pretty brave pest. And sort of nice, too."

Liz gave a big, happy smile.

"Okay, silly," she said. "You can call me pest if you want."

David hoisted her up and galloped off down the beach.

"You're a heavy pest. You're a wet pest. You're my sister pest. You're the best pest there is," he chanted.

They laughed and laughed all the way home.